JOHN
WINTHROP
COLONIAL GOVERNOR OF MASSACHUSETTS

SPECIAL LIVES IN HISTORY THAT BECOME

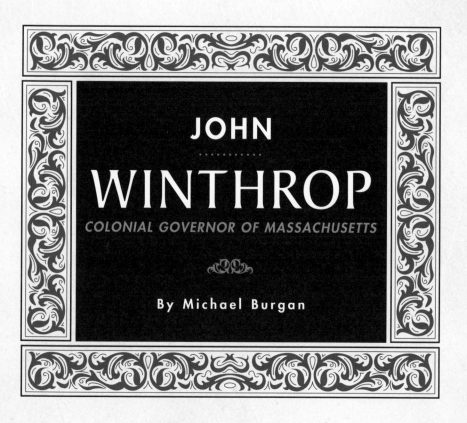

JOHN
WINTHROP
COLONIAL GOVERNOR OF MASSACHUSETTS

By Michael Burgan

Content Adviser: John W. Ifkovic, Ph.D.,
Professor of History, Westfield State College

Reading Adviser: Rosemary G. Palmer, Ph.D.,
Department of Literacy, College of Education,
Boise State University

COMPASS POINT BOOKS  MINNEAPOLIS, MINNESOTA

Compass Point Books
3109 West 50th Street, #115
Minneapolis, MN 55410

Visit Compass Point Books on the Internet at *www.compasspointbooks.com*
or e-mail your request to *custserv@compasspointbooks.com*

Editor: Sue Vander Hook
Page Production: The Design Lab
Photo Researcher: Svetlana Zhurkin
Cartographer: XNR Productions, Inc.
Library Consultant: Kathleen Baxter

Art Director: Jaime Martens
Creative Director: Keith Griffin
Editorial Director: Carol Jones
Managing Editor: Catherine Neitge

Library of Congress Cataloging-in-Publication Data
Burgan, Michael
  John Winthrop: colonial governor of Massachusetts / by Michael Burgan
  p. cm—(Signature lives)
  Includes bibliographical references and index.
  ISBN 0-7565-1591-2 (hardcover)
  1. John Winthrop, 1588–1649—Juvenile literature. 2. Governors—
Massachusetts—Biography—Juvenile literature. 3. Puritans—
Massachusetts—Biography—Juvenile literature. 4. Massachusetts—
History—Colonial period, ca. 1600-1775—Juvenile literature. I. Title.
II. Series.
  F67.W79B87 2006
  974.4'02092—dc22   2005025210

Signature Lives

COLONIAL AMERICA

As they arrived in North America, European colonists found an expansive land of potential riches and unlimited opportunities. Many left their homes in the Old World seeking religious and political freedom. Others sought the chance to build a better life for themselves. The effort to settle a vast new land was not easy, and the colonists faced struggles over land, religion, and freedoms. But despite the many conflicts, great cities emerged, new industries developed, and the foundation for a new type of government was laid. Meanwhile, Native Americans fought to keep their ancestral lands and traditions alive in a rapidly changing world that became as new to them as it was to the colonists.

Table of Contents

1 A City Upon a Hill

❦

John Winthrop opened his journal and dated it July 2, 1630. He briefly wrote:

> *My son, Henry Winthrop, was drowned at Salem.*

That's all he said about the death of his second son on that tragic summer day. Twenty-two-year-old Henry had volunteered to swim across the river to fetch an abandoned canoe. Cramps gripped the young man, and he drowned before he could reach shore. There was more bad news that day.

Winthrop wrote:

> *The* Talbot *arrived there. She had lost fourteen passengers.*

John Winthrop's fleet of 11 ships began arriving in Boston Harbor in 1630.

The *Talbot* was not the only ship in Winthrop's fleet that suffered casualties. Other passengers died on the difficult voyage across the Atlantic Ocean.

Winthrop and hundreds of other Puritans had now been in North America for just 18 days. They were there to start a new colony—a place where they could escape religious persecution and establish a community based on their spiritual beliefs.

They were in North America, but their citizenship was in England. Three months before on England's shore, they had boarded 11 ships packed with their animals and possessions. They were ready to leave their homeland.

Winthrop and his three sons were onboard the wooden flagship *Arbella*—the leader of the fleet. The ships bobbed in English waters for several days as they waited for the weather to clear. It had taken six months for Winthrop to prepare for this voyage. So a few more days didn't matter. It had been a hard decision to sell his home and property and leave his wife and other children behind.

Many people gave up a great deal to make this trip. But they were determined to leave England. These English merchants, wealthy investors, and their families wanted to start a colony. It was going to be more than just another English settlement in the New World. It would be a community where they could worship God as they pleased.

Many Puritans set sail from the River Thames in London for their voyage to the New World.

Winthrop firmly believed God had given him and the other Puritans a unique opportunity—to be an example to the world. The Puritans felt called by God to be a model of the proper way to live—according to the rules set down in the Bible. Winthrop was an educated and deeply religious man with the ability to lead and encourage people.

Although he was not a minister, Winthrop preached a sermon to his fellow travelers. He called it "A Model of Christian Charity." His words reminded the Puritans of their purpose—to purify the Church of England by establishing a colony that would be an example for all people.

Using an idea from Matthew 5:14 in the Bible, he proclaimed:

> *For we must consider that we shall be as a City upon a Hill. The eyes of all people are upon us.*

Then he warned them that if they failed their calling, the whole world would know:

John Winthrop (1588-1649)

> *[I]f we shall deal falsely with our God in this work we have undertaken, and so cause him to withdraw his present help from us, we shall be made a story and a by-word through the world. We shall open the mouths of enemies to speak evil of the ways of God, ... We shall shame the faces of many of God's worthy servants, ... till we be consumed out of the good land whither we are a going.*

Winthrop's sermon also encouraged the Puritans to work together, care for each other, and love one another, if they expected to survive in their new community. To Winthrop, God was the source of charity, or love, and Christians should love each other and help one other. "If one member suffers," he preached, "all suffer with it; if one be in honor, all rejoice with it."

With the *Arbella* in the lead, four of the ships finally left the coast of England. On April 8, 1630, they headed out to the open sea. Strong headwinds and storms often tested the seaworthiness of these wooden vessels. Winthrop and about 400 others were the first to land on a peninsula they called Massachusetts Bay Colony. It would eventually become the state of Massachusetts.

The rest of the 11 ships finally arrived, delivering several hundred more people to the shores of North America. Thousands more would follow over the next few years. Far from England's officials, they could now worship as they wanted and establish their own society. They would live in freedom, away from the

Many people came to the New World from England before John Winthrop. In 1620, a group of Pilgrims established Plymouth Colony. The first Puritans reached Massachusetts around 1625. Another group of Puritans, led by John Endecott, landed in what is now Salem in 1628. That settlement failed, but Endecott served as governor of Massachusetts Bay from 1629 to 1630. Winthrop became governor when he arrived in 1630. Endecott would serve as governor again from 1644 to 1645.

John Winthrop kept a detailed account of his journey from England to Massachusetts in his journal.

Church of England that they disagreed with. They would be far from the king and his religious leaders who had actively pursued them and even executed their friends and loved ones.

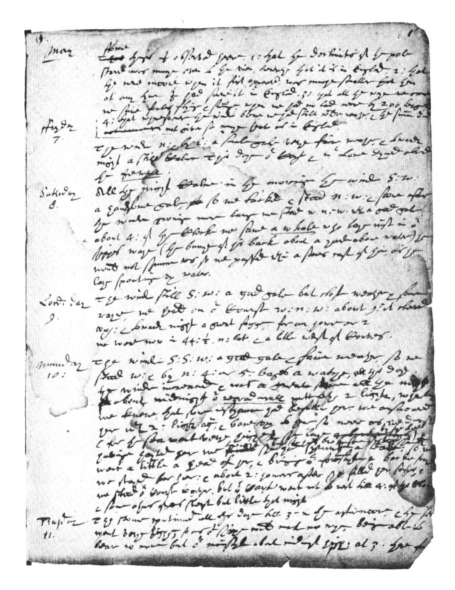

Almost every day, Winthrop wrote in his journal about the events that came to be called the Great Migration. For the next 19 years, he wrote a vivid account of what happened in the Massachusetts Bay Colony. His journals would become three volumes of history, explaining how the seeds of democracy were planted in America. He described a colony that would eventually help shape the government of the United States of America.

For many years, John Winthrop served as governor of Massachusetts Bay Colony. He did his best to rule fairly and make sure the colony survived. This wise and caring man worked hard with his fellow Puritans to establish their city upon a hill. It would one day become the state of Massachusetts.

2 PURITAN CHILD

❧❧❧

John Winthrop was born on January 12, 1588, to a family that was firmly established in Suffolk along the east coast of England. John's grandfather, Adam Winthrop, had purchased land there in 1544. John's father, also named Adam, was a lawyer. His mother, Anne Browne Winthrop, the daughter of a Puritan minister, was now mother of four—John and his three older sisters, Anne, Jane, and Lucy.

They were a wealthy family with a nice home called Groton Manor. They were also very religious people, deeply committed to the teachings of the Bible. The Winthrops belonged to a group that came to be called Puritans because they wanted to purify the government-run Church of England. They believed the church was too much like the

Roman Catholic Church and that it should follow the teachings of Scripture more closely. Although the Puritans didn't give themselves their name, it fit their purpose and how they sought to live a pure life.

The 1500s was not a good time to oppose the Church of England. For nearly 100 years, religious conflict had divided the English people. In 1534, more than 50 years before John was born, King Henry VIII had broken away from the Roman Catholic Church and created a new national church—the Church of England. Henry said the pope was no longer the head of the church, and he declared himself the head.

England's Henry VIII (1491–1547) wanted to break away from the Roman Catholic Church for personal reasons. He wanted to divorce his wife Catherine of Aragon, and the pope wouldn't let him. It was against the rules of the church. Henry was ready to marry a younger woman, Anne Boleyn. He hoped she would give him a son who would become king of England, something Catherine had been unable to do.

When Henry died and his daughter Mary became queen in 1553, religious conflicts increased. Mary quickly changed the official religion back to Catholicism with the pope as the head of the church. She began executing Protestants, the people who had broken away from the Catholic Church.

This queen, aptly called "Bloody Mary," died in 1558, and her sister Elizabeth took over the throne. Queen Elizabeth I returned England to

Churches in England like Westminster Abbey became Protestant when Henry VIII established the Church of England.

the Protestant religion but required English citizens to be members of the Church of England.

John Winthrop grew up during the reign of Queen Elizabeth I and in the midst of ongoing religious conflicts. Some people still wanted England to be a Roman Catholic nation. Others, called Separatists, didn't want a government-run church at all. The Puritans, on the other hand, didn't want to put an end to the Church of England, but they wanted it to change. In spite of the conflicts, the Winthrop family didn't waiver from their Puritan beliefs.

John's father was dedicated to his religious principles, but he was also a prominent English citizen. He worked hard as a lawyer and farmed rye, barley, wheat, and peas on his large estate. He was a member of the gentry, the upper class of England who owned large parcels of land.

The Winthrops' large two-story home was an active place. The family ate and entertained guests on the first floor. There was also a bake house for baking bread and other foods and a small brewery for making beer. Several servants and a huge dog named Grymble were also part of the Winthrop household.

Wealthy farmers in Suffolk, England, often lived in large two-story homes called manors.

Lawyers and ministers often visited Groton Manor to discuss law, religion, and politics. John probably learned a lot from these frequent visitors. But he also learned from his parents, his first teachers, and tutors hired to teach John and his sisters.

Education was important to the Winthrops, and religion was a fundamental part of that education. Puritans taught their children the basics of reading and writing so they could read and study the Bible. John's grandfather Henry Browne once wrote, "The cause of error is the ignorance of God's word."

The Puritans were unusual for their time. They taught both boys and girls how to read and write. Most people believed formal education was important only for boys. John's mother was a highly educated woman. Not only could she read and write English, she also knew Latin and French.

John went to church regularly, where he listened to sermons and studied the Bible. Later, as an adult, he wrote:

> [A]bout ten years of age, I had some notions of God: for in some frighting [something frightening], or danger, I have prayed unto God, and found manifest [clear] answer; ... After I was twelve years old, ... I thought I had more understanding in Divinity [God] than many of my years.

Although school and church kept John busy, he also found time to do other activities. Sometimes he played a game similar to soccer. He learned to fish and shoot a gun and a bow and arrow. Fishing and hunting were important activities—they put food on the table.

When John was 14 years old, it was time for him to go to the university, as most wealthy boys did at that age. In December 1602, he left Groton Manor and went to Cambridge University in Cambridge, England, which his father had attended. There he studied Latin, Greek, and other subjects. He followed a strict schedule that included daily prayers and church services.

John's first year at Cambridge was not easy. He was sick with what he called a lingering fever that "took away the comforts of my life." But it was while he was ill that John's faith deepened as he "took pleasure in drawing nearer to him [God]."

College life brought about many changes for John, but England was also changing. A few months after John arrived at Cambridge, Queen Elizabeth died, and James I became king. Puritans hoped that James might change the Church of England to include their beliefs—the teachings of John Calvin, a Protestant religious leader. Followers of Calvin, called Calvinists, believed God chose a number of people—the elect—who would go to heaven. Nothing they did on Earth would change God's decision. Calvinists believed the elect should still have a strong faith in Jesus as the Son of God and live a pure life according to the standards of the Bible. King James didn't do what the Puritans wanted, however, and the Church of England didn't change.

*John Calvin
(1509–1564)*

In November 1604, John took a break from his classes. He and his friend William Forth took a trip to Great Stambridge, just one county away in Essex, to visit Forth's relatives. During his stay, 16-year-old John met 21-year-old Mary Forth. Five months later, they were married. John permanently left Cambridge and moved to Great Stambridge, where he and Mary lived in her parents' home. Soon they would start a family of their own. ☙

3 RELIGIOUS PERSECUTION

❧❦❧

John and Mary Winthrop were married 10 months when they became parents. They named their son John, after his father. Two years later in 1608, their son Henry was born, followed the next year by another son named Forth.

The Winthrops spent most of their time in Great Stambridge, though they occasionally visited Groton Manor. Winthrop's faith in God was growing during this time. He described his efforts to avoid sin by asking God to "strengthen me against the world, the flesh, and the devil … and increase my faith."

Winthrop's religious beliefs slowly shaped his actions. He gave up activities that were illegal, immoral, or what he considered to be a waste of

John Winthrop led the largest migration of colonists to the New World in 1630.

time. No longer did he hunt birds or play cards. He limited how much he ate since he was tempted to eat more than he thought he needed. Winthrop believed he should spend his time improving himself and thinking about God.

However, Winthrop's time was not spent thinking only about religious matters. At the age of 21, he became a landowner and had to learn the duties of owning property.

In 1609, Winthrop's uncle was about to lose Groton Manor because of legal troubles. Instead, he gave the estate to John to make sure it stayed in the family. After attending some court hearings, Winthrop became the legal owner of Groton Manor. Perhaps his courtroom experience had an effect on him, because two years later he started attending Gray's Inn, a law school in London.

In 1612, John and Mary had another child—a girl named Mary, after her mother. The Winthrops were enjoying their growing family, but over the next three years, they would be struck by several tragedies.

Mary's father died in 1613, and Winthrop began managing the land his father-in-law had owned. The following year, the couple's daughter Anne was born, but she died about a week later. On June 26, 1615, Mary prepared to deliver another baby. The delivery did not go well, and Mary and the baby, also named Anne, both died. They were buried together near the

altar inside the church in Groton.

Puritans taught their children that it was important to study the Bible, pray, and attend church services.

As usual, God was not far from John Winthrop's mind. When Mary's father died, Winthrop wrote that he wanted to "give myself, my life, my [intelligence], my health, my wealth to the service of my God and Savior." He also promised to pray every morning, work hard, and do whatever he thought God directed him to do.

Winthrop wrote very little about his wife. But after her death, he wrote that he remembered the "sweet love" they shared. Just a few months after Mary's death, Winthrop got married again—to Thomasine Clopton. Winthrop described her as a true Puritan

During the 1600s, being a wife and mother was difficult. Many women died giving birth, and many infants died soon after they were born. Even in the healthiest communities, about one child in 10 died before the age of 5. Pregnancy was also surrounded by many superstitions. It was believed that if a pregnant woman were startled by a loud noise, her child would be disfigured. People thought if a hare jumped in front of a woman, her baby might be born with a harelip. Or if the expectant mother looked at the moon, her child might become a sleepwalker.

and praised her "loving and tender regard" for her family. Within a year, however, Thomasine also died during childbirth.

In the middle of his personal difficulties, Winthrop had taken on new public duties. The year before Thomasine died, he was appointed justice of the peace, someone who enforced local laws and sometimes sentenced criminals to jail. He also decided how money would be collected for the poor and kept citizens informed about what their government officials were doing.

Winthrop took his position seriously and believed he had a duty to God and to the community to do what was right. He prayed that he would do his work well and not be tempted to turn his attention to material desires. Some of the other justices weren't devoted to God like Winthrop was. But many other leaders in the community shared his Puritan beliefs.

In 1617, Winthrop became interested in Margaret Tyndal, daughter of a wealthy Puritan family. One of her relatives thought Winthrop was not rich enough to marry Margaret. Winthrop argued in letters to Margaret that marriage was not about wealth. Two people should marry because they held similar views of God, he said. "Love bred our fellowship," he wrote. "Let love continue it." In 1618 they were married.

Winthrop continued to serve as justice of the peace and run the family estate. He met with his farm

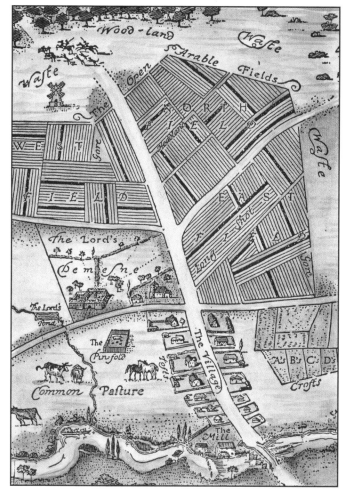

Typical layout of an English farm in the 1600s

workers and told them what to do each day. In the spring, the men prepared the earth and planted seeds. During the summer, they weeded and watered the fields, and in the fall they harvested crops. Margaret, meanwhile, worked with their household servants to make sure the family had good food, nice clothes, and a clean home.

In 1619, John and Margaret had their first child— Stephen—followed by Adam a year later. They would eventually have eight children, but only four of them would live past infancy. Margaret served as schoolteacher for their children and for John's four children from his first marriage. The children also attended grammar school in the area. The younger John went to Bury St. Edmunds School in Suffolk. In a typical school of the time, students met at 6 A.M. for breakfast, followed by prayers. They learned to read and write Latin and Greek and studied the works of ancient writers. Classes lasted until 5 P.M., and then students studied at home during the evenings and on Saturdays.

At times, Winthrop considered moving his large family out of England. "I wish oft God would open a way to settle me in Ireland, if it might be for his glory," he wrote. Protestant churches there didn't look down on Puritans or their ideas.

Winthrop didn't move to Ireland. Instead, he began working for the government of England. He used his legal training to write laws that would be presented to Parliament, England's legislative body. One of the laws he wrote protected the rights of Puritans, but Parliament didn't pass it. The government was watching Puritans more and preventing them from

Parliament, England's law-making body, was first established by King Henry III in the 13th century.

worshipping as they chose, even in private.

Winthrop also wrote a document about Roman Catholics, who were increasing in number. In it he stated that Puritans hoped "some fundamental law may be made to remove all their children from them" so they could be taught Protestant beliefs.

A year later, in 1625, a new king—Charles I—took over the throne of England. Soon, Charles began

King Charles I (1600–1649) with his queen, Henrietta Maria and two of their children

allowing more Catholic traditions and rituals in the Protestant Church of England. His Roman Catholic wife probably had some influence over him when it came to religious matters.

Now the Puritans faced new problems and a new enemy. Charles chose Bishop William Laud as his top religious adviser. Laud strongly opposed the teachings of John Calvin. He wanted the government to have more control over what went on in the Church of England. Laud and the king began to crack down on Puritans who did not follow all the rules of the Anglican church.

Bishop William Laud worked with King Charles I to set the rules for the Church of England.

Charles and Laud insisted that Puritans and other Protestants worship according to the standards of the Church of England. Ministers who disobeyed were punished. The religious disputes spilled over into Parliament. Some important members of Parliament were Puritans, and they were not pleased with the decisions the king and Laud were making. Lawmakers argued with Charles over religion and taxes. They argued about money and disagreed on whom Charles chose as his closest advisers. Parliament was growing more upset with the rules Charles was making for the church. A battle for power had begun that would go on for many years.

In 1626, Winthrop ran for election to the House of Commons, the branch of Parliament whose members were elected by the people. Winthrop lost the election but stayed involved in local government.

In 1627, he was appointed to a court that managed land controlled by the government of England. The job required him to travel to London about four times a year. Winthrop wrote to his wife that this job brought "success beyond our expectation." It was a well-respected position and paid well besides.

Soon, however, he grew tired of traveling. It was expensive living in two places. He debated whether he should buy a home in London or give up his important job. Part of him wanted to return to his simple country life, yet he knew his family needed the money that his job provided.

Winthrop was also grappling with family issues. His son Henry often lived a wild life. His parents did not approve of his lifestyle and didn't think he was quite as bright as his brothers. So they encouraged him to go overseas. The Winthrops hoped his journey would teach him useful skills.

In December 1626, Henry set sail for the island

of Barbados, in the West Indies. But after three years and a failed business venture, he returned to England and ran up some debts before getting married. The elder Winthrop told his wife Margaret they could not support Henry and his new wife, and they refused to let them live at Groton Manor.

His son John, now in his early 20s, quit law school to join the navy. Winthrop was not pleased with his decision. Then in 1628, the younger John talked about traveling to the New World—to a place called Massachusetts Bay Colony. Puritans had started settling there a few years before. Winthrop told his son he didn't want him to settle in Massachusetts. His son respected his wishes and decided not to go.

John Winthrop Jr. was the oldest child of John and Mary Winthrop.

Around this time, Winthrop came down with a serious illness that he blamed partly on his "use and love of tobacco." He stopped using tobacco and recovered from his illness. Then he suffered another tragedy—his mother died. Over the last few years, Winthrop had suffered many troubles, but he said that

35

one thing remained constant in his life—his faith in God. He wrote to Margaret in 1629 that it was a great favor from God that they enjoyed "so much comfort and peace in these so evil and declining times."

The evil times Winthrop was concerned about were the mounting problems Puritans were experiencing in England. Conflict between the king and Parliament was still going on. Finally, in March 1629, the king shut down Parliament and gave full support to religious leaders who were against the Puritans and their beliefs. Laud hired men to watch what Puritan ministers were doing. If they didn't wear the proper clothing in church or use government-approved prayers, they were fined, denied the right to preach, or publicly punished.

Winthrop again started thinking about leaving England to get away from the persecution. Now, like his son, he considered going to the New World. He was already a member of the New England Company, a group of merchants and businessmen who wanted to start a colony in North America.

In 1629, the company asked the king to sign a charter to give the group control of land in Massachusetts. The king granted the charter to the group who now called itself the Massachusetts Bay Company. Somehow, the writers of the document left out any details about where the leaders of the colony had to live. The charter didn't state that the

governor and officers of the company had to remain in England. This would later prove to be a fortunate mistake for the colony.

Members of the group were Puritans, and they were interested in the colony being more than merely

Throughout the 1600s, Puritans were locked in the public pillory, or stocks, to humiliate and persecute them for their faith.

a business venture. They believed it could be a safe religious haven for persecuted Puritans. In Suffolk and nearby counties, other Puritans heard about the plan to send settlers to Massachusetts. Some eagerly wanted to go to the New World, while others disapproved of the plan. They reminded Winthrop of ships that had sunk trying to cross the Atlantic Ocean, and they told him how difficult life was for settlers who had already gone to North America. New World colonists had sent back word that food was scarce and the Indians sometimes hostile.

One of Winthrop's friends told him that at the age of 41, he was too old for such an adventure. Crossing the Atlantic to establish a new home is "for young men, that can endure all pains and hunger," his friend wrote. Still, Winthrop thought about making the difficult journey.

In July, Winthrop and a group of Puritans met with leaders of the Massachusetts Bay Company. Two Puritan ministers—John Cotton and Thomas Hooker—were there. They were being pressured by the government and Bishop Laud to make their churches conform to the rules of the Church of England. Now these men discussed how they could make the colony in Massachusetts a center for Puritan teachings.

After the meeting, Winthrop wrote a list of reasons why Puritans should go to Massachusetts. Puritan ministers could teach their beliefs to the Indians and prevent them from becoming members of the Roman Catholic Church, he wrote. Puritans were concerned that French priests already in North America were encouraging Indians to become Catholics. Winthrop also believed Puritans would be saved from the punishment he believed God was going to pour

For many years, Puritans had come before English monarchs to request church reform.

John Winthrop was governor of Massachusetts Bay Colony, one of the original 13 North American colonies.

out on the people of Europe. He added to the list that Puritans could earn an honest living there. In England, workers were often forced to break the law or go against their religious beliefs if they wanted to keep their jobs. "It is almost impossible for a good

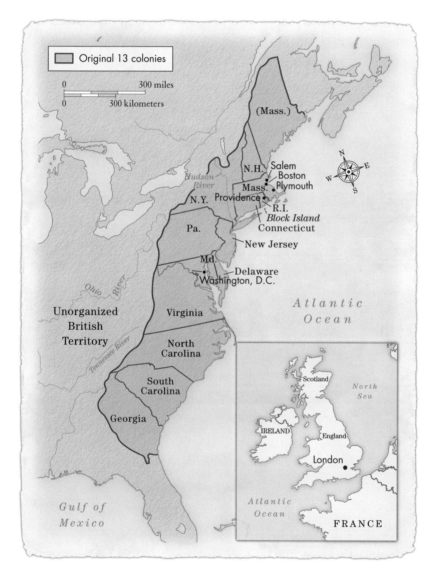

and upright man to maintain his charge and live comfortably," Winthrop wrote.

On August 26, 1629, Winthrop finalized his decision—he would go to America. He and 11 other Puritan leaders signed a document called the Cambridge Agreement. They agreed to work together to bring their families and supplies to Massachusetts. Since the royal charter didn't require leaders of the colony to remain in England, all the leaders would go. The residents of the Massachusetts Bay Colony would have fewer ties to England and more control over their civil affairs than any other settlers in North America.

The next step was to elect a governor for the colony. Company officials chose Winthrop. They had "received extraordinary great commendations of ... his integrity [honesty]" and that he was "very well fitted and accomplished for the place of Governor."

Winthrop welcomed the new task before him. He wrote:

I have assurance that my charge is of the Lord and that he has called me to this work.

Now Winthrop made preparations to take hundreds of Puritans to their new home in the New World. ❧

4 A COLONY IN THE NEW WORLD

Chapter

෬ඥ෨

For the next six months, Winthrop and other leaders of the Massachusetts Bay Company prepared for the voyage to Massachusetts. Although the company already had a small settlement in Salem, this Puritan migration would be the largest yet to sail to North America. Winthrop had to find enough ships to carry about 700 colonists with their animals and belongings.

The new settlement would need carpenters, brickmakers, blacksmiths, and men with military experience. Many of the people who decided to go were friends and neighbors of Winthrop who lived in Suffolk. Others simply heard about the plan and decided they would risk the trip to the New World. Entire families decided to go together and bring along their servants.

John Winthrop stands on the deck of the Arbella *off the shore of Salem, Massachusetts, before landing in 1630.*

Massachusetts Bay
Colony, 1630–1686

Map shows
present-day boundaries.

Maine

United
Kingdom

Ireland   Edwardston
Cambridge
London
Great Stambridge
to Salem

Atlantic
Ocean

North
Sea

Vermont   New
Hampshire

Merrimack River

Connecticut River

Massachusetts   Salem

from England

Algonquians

Charlestown
Shawmut
(Boston)

Atlantic
Ocean

Plymouth

Pequots

Providence

Connecticut   Rhode
Island

Block
Island

Atlantic
Ocean

New York

0   30 miles
0   30 kilometers

N
W   E
S

*John Winthrop
lived in Suffolk,
England, before
migrating to
the New World
to serve as
governor of the
Massachusetts
Bay Colony.*

During this busy time of preparation, Winthrop also had to handle his personal affairs. He needed to sell the family estate and say goodbye to friends and relatives. Margaret was expecting another child and decided to stay in England until after the baby was born. Henry, Stephen, and Adam would sail with their father. The other children—John, Forth, Mary, Deane, and Samuel—would stay with their mother in England. Winthrop and his wife saw little of each other in the months before he left England, but they wrote each other often.

In one letter, Margaret said, "My thoughts are now on our great change and alteration of our course here." Yet her feelings for Winthrop were clear: "I know not how to express my love to [you]." During one of their last visits together, they promised to set aside two hours each week to think about each other and pray for one another. "We shall meet in spirit," Winthrop wrote, "until we meet in person."

In March 1630, Winthrop and hundreds of Puritans were ready for the long trip to Massachusetts. Eleven ships prepared to sail from three ports. John Winthrop sailed from Southampton on the *Arbella*. The large wooden ship weighed 350 tons (315 metric tons) and carried 24 cannons to fight off pirates or other enemies that might threaten the fleet.

John Winthrop and the other Puritans needed food for their voyage to the New World and the first few months in Massachusetts Bay Colony. They also needed seeds, farm animals, building supplies, weapons, and ammunition. The final list of cargo for the Arbella and 10 other ships included 240 cows, 60 horses, eight cannons, more than 100 muskets, much woolen cloth, and various kitchen tools.

Three other ships anchored off the coast with the *Arbella* for about a week and waited for other ships in the harbor to set sail. Tired of waiting, the four

John Winthrop spent a lot of time writing. He wrote a series of papers on religious and political topics. He also wrote many letters, and some have survived until today. His most important writings were his journals. Winthrop began the first of three books while waiting for the Arbella to leave England. For the next 19 years, he wrote down details of his public life in Massachusetts Bay Colony. He described the colony's politics and its relations with both Native Americans and neighboring colonies. Winthrop's handwriting was not easy to read, but later historians carefully studied his journals to learn about life in the first two decades of colonial Massachusetts. His journals offer one of the most complete views of political life during those times.

ships left their spot on March 29 but anchored again for several days while they waited for the weather to clear. Finally, on April 8, 1630, the four ships set sail from England and headed for the open waters of the Atlantic Ocean. The other ships in the fleet would follow soon.

Winthrop had already started writing in his journal by then. Almost every day, he recorded the progress of the ships and the activities of the Puritans.

In one entry, he described how they saw eight ships approaching. Fearing they were pirates, the men on the *Arbella* prepared for battle. Winthrop wrote:

> *All the hamackoes [hammocks] were taken down, and our [gun]powder chests and fireworks [guns] made ready.*

Everyone was relieved to finally learn that the ships were friendly.

For most of the trip, the weather was cool. At times, severe storms tossed the ships about, causing one

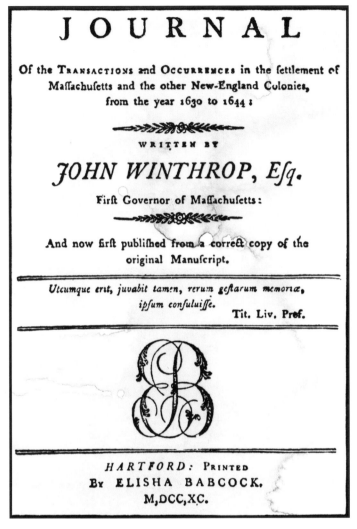

JOURNAL

Of the TRANSACTIONS and OCCURRENCES in the settlement of
Massachusetts and the other New-England Colonies,
from the year 1630 to 1644:

WRITTEN BY

JOHN WINTHROP, Esq.

First Governor of Massachusetts:

And now first published from a correct copy of the
original Manuscript.

*Utcumque erit, juvabit tamen, rerum gestarum memoria,
ipsum consuluisse.*
Tit. Liv. Pref.

HARTFORD: PRINTED
By ELISHA BABCOCK.
M,DCC,XC.

Title page of the original issue of John Winthrop's Journal, *which is considered the main source for the history of Massachusetts in the 1630s and 1640s*

ship to fall far behind the others. Winthrop noted the death of two servants on another ship, and he described how two young men were punished for fighting. Most of the young people onboard, however, behaved well, he wrote.

On June 12, the *Arbella* approached the coast of

Massachusetts near Salem. John Endecott, Puritan leader and governor of the colony there, came out in a small boat to meet them. He invited Winthrop and other leaders to come on shore and have dinner with him. Other passengers went to nearby Cape Ann to pick strawberries.

John Winthrop and hundreds of other Puritans landed on the shore of Salem, Massachusetts, on June 12, 1630.

Winthrop soon heard about the many difficulties the Salem settlers had already faced. About 80 people had died during the past winter, and many were still

sick and weak from lack of food. They lived in shacks and wigwams on the edge of unexplored forests full of wild animals. They often felt threatened by neighboring Indian tribes. They had few words of encouragement for Winthrop's group.

More bad news came as the other ships in Winthrop's fleet arrived during the following weeks. Seventy cattle had died onboard one ship, and on another, the people were nearly starved. On yet another ship, 14 passengers had died.

The new colonists, however, didn't let the difficulties stop them from establishing their colony. After searching the area, Winthrop chose a spot—the bay area around Charlestown. In September, the group set to work building a colony that they believed would survive.

Winthrop set an example for the rest of the Puritans with his hard work. A report written in London described how he "fell to work with his own hands, and thereby so encouraged the rest that there was not an idle person to be found." The settlers erected houses, dug caves in the hillsides, and put roofs on underground cellars.

Winthrop sent one of the ships—the *Lyon*— back to England to buy more food for the coming winter. He dashed off a quick letter to his son John in England, asking him to bring food when he came. Occasionally, he wrote to his wife explaining that he had been too busy to think of her at the agreed upon time each week.

Before long, Winthrop realized that settling in Charlestown was not a good idea. After two settlers died, possibly from contaminated water, he began to look for another location for the colony. The colonists needed a place with an abundant supply of clean drinking water. In early October, about 150 settlers moved across the harbor to another peninsula where there was plenty of clean water.

The local Indians called it Shawmut, but the colonists named their new home Boston in honor of an English town with that name. Other settlers established their own towns nearby. For a time, the Puritans lived in tents or wigwams—like the nearby Algonquian Indians—until they could build more permanent wooden homes.

While establishing his new colony, Winthrop faced a number of personal tragedies. His son Henry had drowned 18 days after they arrived, but there were more heartaches.

Death was common during the early days of the Massachusetts Bay Colony. Winthrop wrote in his journal about cattle and other farm animals being killed by wolves. Food was scarce, and by the end of November, seven of Winthrop's servants had died.

The first winter in Massachusetts Bay Colony began with a fierce storm just before Christmas.

A windmill overlooked the first houses at Boston in the 1630s.

People suffered frostbite and endured temperatures colder than any they had experienced in England. Some people started fires in their homes to keep warm, but many of the thatched roofs caught on fire, and the houses burned down.

But Winthrop was determined that the Puritans' establishment would not crumble. He arranged for the settlers to buy and trade corn and land with the nearby Indian tribes. It was also important that everyone continue to work hard and do their part to survive.

Winthrop traded goods for land from nearby Indian tribes.

In February 1631, the settlers saw a welcome sight. The *Lyon* had arrived with a cargo full of food and supplies. Winthrop did not hesitate to order a day of thanksgiving and prayer to thank God for the much needed provisions.

The first winter was almost over, but the colonists had paid a high price. More than 200 people died, and 80 more decided to return to England when the *Lyon* set sail on its return voyage. About 200 others left the colony to settle in other spots.

Governor Winthrop had guided the citizens of

the colony through their first dark days and months. In the years to come, many more settlers would join them as they continued to establish Massachusetts Bay Colony. ❧

5 POLITICAL BATTLES

Chapter

❧⧼❧

The king of England had given the Massachusetts Bay Company complete control of the colony, as long as it didn't break the laws of England. But the great distance between England and Massachusetts made it hard for King Charles or his aides to know exactly what the growing community of more than 1,000 Puritans was doing. In the meantime, the colony was setting up its own form of government. Governor Winthrop was advised by a council called his assistants. Second-in-command to Winthrop was Deputy Governor Thomas Dudley.

Leaders of the colony met four times a year at the General Court, a government body that passed laws and handled colony business. The governor, deputy governor, and the assistants were in charge

Bible reading was an important part of colonial life for the Puritans of Massachusetts Bay Colony.

of enforcing laws. The General Court had met for the first time in October 1630, about three months after their ships landed. At that meeting, Winthrop and his assistants declared that about 100 men in the community would be freemen, people who were allowed to vote. To qualify as a freeman, one had to be a mature male and a member of the church. A freeman had to testify that he had experienced God's grace through a life-changing spiritual experience. Church leaders confirmed each freeman's religious conversion. As voting members of the colony, freemen elected the governor's assistants. The assistants in turn elected the deputy governor and the governor.

When the General Court met for the second time, more people were allowed to be freemen. In fact, all males—except servants—were admitted as freemen, as long as they met the spiritual qualifications. Most men in the colony belonged to a local church and could testify of their religious transformation, so many became voting freemen. By the following year, freemen were allowed to directly elect the governor and his deputy governor, as well.

Winthrop hoped that if people had some power over how the colony was governed, they would obey the laws and work for the common good. Yet Winthrop and others didn't think everyone should vote or that just anyone could serve in government. The Puritans considered some people naturally

Several Puritan colonists walk to church.

better than others. These "betters," as they were called, had been chosen by God. People with less power were expected to respect their authority. This distinction applied to men and women, too—God made men superior to women, they taught.

Some residents grumbled about how Winthrop governed the colony. One person who criticized him harshly was Dudley. Quick to anger and rigid in his beliefs, Dudley thought Winthrop was too lenient with people who were weak in their Puritan beliefs. He also thought the governor should always consult him and the assistants about decisions. Dudley was also angry with Winthrop for not building his home in Newtown, now known as Cambridge. Dudley had

Thomas Dudley (1576–1653), deputy governor of Massachusetts Bay Colony

built his home there, hoping that Winthrop and the assistants would also live there. He wanted Newtown to become the major town in the settlement.

Disagreements between the two men had a personal side, too. During the first year in Massachusetts, Dudley loaned corn to some of the settlers rather than give it to them, as Winthrop did. To make matters worse, Dudley now expected them to pay him back with more corn than he had loaned them. Winthrop thought Dudley's actions were unchristian. He also thought Dudley's home was too fancy. Puritans believed in living simply and devoting their life to God, not showing off their wealth or status.

In the midst of the conflict between the two men, Winthrop celebrated a happy occasion. In November 1631, he was reunited with his wife. Margaret arrived in Massachusetts with her mother, their youngest son Samuel, and Winthrop's oldest son John and his wife Margaret. But other members of the family weren't there. Their 8-year-old son Deane had stayed in England. They planned for him to come later. Winthrop's 20-year-old son Forth had died in England the year before. Then there was more sad news about their daughter Anne, who was born in England after Winthrop left. He had never seen his youngest daughter, and now she had died on the ocean voyage.

Despite the deaths of his loved ones, Winthrop was glad to be reunited with at least some of his family. They arrived amid a huge celebration in the colony. The settlers were thanking their governor for helping the colony survive its first difficult year.

Winthrop and his wife were now able to enjoy each other's company once again. They lived in the stone house Winthrop had built along the Mystic River in what is now Somerville. Winthrop continued to govern the colony, make its laws, and enforce what he felt would be God's just punishment. However, some people still thought he was too lenient, showing too much mercy for people who committed crimes.

John Winthrop served 12 terms as governor of Massachusetts Bay Colony.

Dudley was still his main critic.

Tensions between the two men became intense. Finally, in August 1632, they argued publicly. Dudley challenged Winthrop's right to make decisions on his own. Winthrop replied that he only had "whatsoever power belonged to a governor by common law or the statutes." Then "the deputy rose up in great fury and passion and the governor grew very hot also, so as they both fell into bitterness," Winthrop wrote in his journal. Winthrop apologized to the community for mistakes he had made, and he tried to end his quarrel with Dudley. The two men somehow continued to

Winthrop and Dudley quarreled publicly over how to govern the Massachusetts Bay Colony.

work together, although they still disagreed on how to run the colony.

By 1634, some residents of Massachusetts were again upset with the way Winthrop was ruling. Some agreed with Dudley that Winthrop made too many decisions on his own. Others thought he should give out harsher punishments for people who broke the law or went against Puritan teachings. Winthrop tried to defend himself by explaining that Massachusetts was a new society with new people arriving all the time. He said he wanted to be patient with people who didn't know the laws or had trouble finding work. But Winthrop also said "he would be ready to take up a stricter course."

Most people weren't satisfied with his answer. That year, the freemen elected Dudley as their governor. Winthrop was elected deputy governor to serve under Dudley. Winthrop focused on local affairs in Boston, but he also played a part in one of the first great political battles in America. On one side of the battle was the government of Massachusetts Bay Colony. On the other side was Roger Williams, who had arrived in Massachusetts in 1631 onboard the *Lyon*.

Williams first lived in Salem and then moved to Plymouth. Wherever he went, he seemed to get into trouble for his beliefs. Although originally a Puritan, he became a devout Separatist by the time he reached

Massachusetts. In Plymouth, he upset some people when he criticized Puritans for attending the Church of England when they visited England. He believed Separatists as well as Puritans should completely cut themselves off from that church.

Williams also believed that the government of England did not have a right to claim land in North America and then give it to settlers. He believed the land still belonged to the Indians. The English could claim it only if the Indians chose to sell it, he argued. Winthrop, however, did not want to hear any argument that the Puritans didn't have a legal claim to their land.

Roger Williams had good relations with the Indian tribes in the area of Massachusetts Bay Colony. His friendship with Massasoit, chief of the Wampanoags, was so good that they entered into a friendly treaty. Williams did missionary work among the tribes and eventually wrote A Key Into the Languages of America, a book about the Wampanoag Indians and their language.

Winthrop and members of the General Court ordered Williams to take back what he said and swear his loyalty to the king. Williams would not take it back. Church affairs and civil affairs should be kept separate, he proclaimed. He also verbally attacked church leaders in Boston, who refused to read a letter he wrote to their congregations on these issues.

In October 1635, Williams made the last of several appearances before the General Court, which banished him from the

Roger Williams left Massachusetts Bay Colony in the middle of winter after he was exiled by the General Court.

Massachusetts Bay Colony. In January 1636, he headed to land east of Plymouth and founded the town of Providence. Later, Williams would help make it into the colony of Rhode Island. As its leader, he would promise residents the freedom to worship as they chose. He would keep separate the issues of the church and the colony. Massachusetts Bay, meanwhile, kept its government and church closely connected, just as Winthrop wanted. ❧

6 Chapter

AT WAR WITH THE PEQUOTS

෨ඐ෧

Roger Williams had been a threat to the Massachusetts Puritans, but they also faced threats outside
the community. For the most part, Indians in eastern
Massachusetts got along well with the colonists.
However, the Puritans sometimes feared the Indians.
The Indians, on the other hand, felt outnumbered by
the arrival of thousands of colonists.

For a while, the colonists and Indians had good
relations. Each side benefited from trading with the
other. The English had things the Indians wanted,
such as tools, pots, and cloth. The Indians offered the
settlers furs and colored beads called wampum that
were used as money in the region.

Winthrop had first met an Indian on the *Arbella* in
1630, while waiting to come ashore. He wrote in his

*Native Americans welcomed the Puritans with a gift of fish when
they arrived at the Massachusetts Bay Colony in the 1630s.*

journal, "An Indian came aboard us and lay there all night." Over the next few years, Winthrop met with leaders of various tribes in the region and tried to establish good relations. He dined with Chickabot, the sachem, or chief, of the Massachusett Indians. Later, Winthrop had a suit made for Chickabot, who gave him two beaver skins in return.

In 1631, the Narragansett tribe had met with Winthrop, hoping to convince him to send settlers there. One sachem offered Winthrop 80 beaver skins

Governor John Winthrop meets with a Narragansett Indian warrior.

a year if the Puritans farmed his lands. Winthrop said no, believing that the sachem really wanted the Puritans' help in a dispute the Narragansett tribe was having with the Pequot tribe. The governor did not want to get involved.

Three years later, the Pequots came to Massachusetts, seeking an alliance with the Puritans. Winthrop wrote that the Pequots "desired so much our friendship … because they were now in war with the Narragansett." The Puritans and the Pequots agreed to trade with each other, and the leaders of Massachusetts Bay convinced the Pequots and their enemies to end their war.

Relations between the Pequots and Puritans, however, soon soured. In 1634, English sea captain John Stone was killed by members of the Pequot tribe. The Pequots refused to turn over his murderers, as they had promised. Then the trade the two sides had hoped for never developed. In 1636, the Puritans heard that the Pequots were planning a war against them. That year, the younger John Winthrop also met with the Indians. He returned skins and jewelry they had given the Puritans, a sign that their treaty of friendship was over.

Soon after, an English trader named John Oldham was found dead on his ship near Block Island off the Atlantic Coast. Soon, the Narragansetts convinced the Puritans that Oldham's murderers had ties to the Pequots. Winthrop and members of a special government council decided the colony would have to punish the Pequots for Oldham's death and for refusing to turn over Stone's murderers.

Under the command of John Endecott, the Massachusetts Bay Colony sent 90 soldiers to Block Island. After a brief battle between the colonists and Indian warriors, the Indians fled the island. Endecott and his men then burned the Indians' wigwams and cornfields before sailing to the main Pequot village outside Saybrook. There, they burned Indian homes and fields before returning to Boston.

The war, however, was not over. In the spring of 1637, the Pequots attacked Wethersfield, a Puritan settlement on the Connecticut River. Soon, the colonies of Connecticut, Massachusetts Bay, and Plymouth organized an army to fight the Pequots. Fighting with the colonists were the Narragansetts and Mohegans, longtime foes of the Pequots.

In May, these combined forces attacked the main Pequot settlement

> *The Pequots are an Algonquian Indian tribe. After the Pequot War of 1636–1637, the surviving members of the tribe were forced to live under the control of the Mohegan and Narragansett tribes. Some of them were sold into slavery. During the 1970s, people who could trace their family roots to the Pequots began to rebuild their tribe. Today, the Pequots once again control much of their former lands in Connecticut. A casino they manage makes them one of the wealthiest Indian nations in the United States.*

Colonists attacked and set fire to the main Pequot village in 1637.

from two sides. Eventually, they set fire to the village. As residents tried to flee the flames, Mohegan troops outside the village killed them. About 700 Pequots, mostly women, children, and the elderly, died that day. The fighting went on for some time, but the Pequots eventually began to surrender. Finally, they gave up completely. With that victory, Massachusetts Bay never faced another threat from the Pequots.

When the war ended, Winthrop was once again the governor of the colony. He and the other leaders ordered a day of thanksgiving for the settlers' victory. Winthrop was glad the war was over, but Massachusetts Bay now faced a different kind of battle—trouble within its own colony. ꙮ

7 CONFLICT IN THE COLONY

❧❦❧

The problem within Massachusetts Bay had begun with the arrival of new colonists in 1634 and 1635. These settlers had a deep faith in Jesus Christ, like other Puritans, but some of their ideas went against what Winthrop and the other leaders believed. Soon, a debate began over religion and politics.

These new arrivals believed that part of God called the Holy Spirit lived inside true Christians. With God's presence inside them, they believed they didn't have to study the Bible for instructions on how to live. True believers didn't have to constantly watch how they acted or check their beliefs, they claimed. The Holy Spirit would guide them. Most Puritans disagreed. They thought it was important for all Christians to watch their own actions and study the

Anne Hutchinson stood before the General Court on trial for teaching non-Puritan beliefs.

Bible daily—just as Winthrop and many others had done throughout their lives.

To Winthrop, the idea that people did not have to study God's Word or try to obey God's laws was a threat to the Puritan community. Obeying the teachings of the Bible was how people showed they were God's elect—the "visible saints," as the Puritans called themselves. Winthrop and others believed these new thinkers were going against God's laws. They gave them an appropriate name— Antinomians—a word that means "against laws."

John Wheelwright (1592–1679) shared similar ideas with Anne Hutchinson and was eventually banished from the colony.

As Antinomian teachings spread, many Puritans wanted Winthrop to crush the Antinomians and their beliefs. This group was led by Thomas Shepard, a newcomer to Massachusetts and minister of the church in Newtown.

The most outspoken Antinomians were Anne and William Hutchinson, Anne's brother-in-law John Wheelwright, and Henry Vane. In May 1636, Vane was elected governor of the colony and used his position to encourage Antinomian beliefs.

Winthrop wrote about the Antinomian crisis in October 1636. Anne Hutchinson, "a woman of a ready wit and bold spirit," was causing trouble in Boston. Hutchinson attended the same church as Winthrop, but she was holding weekly meetings at her home to talk about Antinomian beliefs.

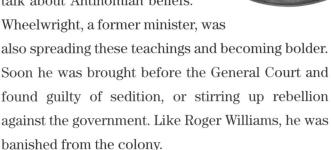

Wheelwright, a former minister, was also spreading these teachings and becoming bolder. Soon he was brought before the General Court and found guilty of sedition, or stirring up rebellion against the government. Like Roger Williams, he was banished from the colony.

Henry Vane (1613–1662) was elected governor of Massachusetts Bay Colony in 1636.

Public discussions about the Antinomians sometimes turned ugly. "All men's mouths were full" of the arguments on both sides, Winthrop wrote. He clearly opposed the Antinomians, but equally as troubling was the conflict the crisis was creating in the General Court.

In May 1637, the voters of Massachusetts Bay Colony once again needed to elect a governor. Would they reelect Vane or elect Winthrop again? The election was marred by anger. One resident wanted to present a petition to the General Court, protesting the treatment of John Wheelwright. Vane supported him, but Winthrop, the deputy governor, argued that the election had to take place before the court could meet. The issue was finally put to the voters, who decided to hold the election first. Winthrop was elected governor. Obviously, most people hoped he could end the Antinomian crisis.

Soon after the election, Vane left Massachusetts, but the problems in the colony were just beginning. Anne Hutchinson continued to hold meetings in her home, sometimes drawing as many as 80 people. She talked about the Holy Spirit coming to true believers and attacked Puritan ministers who opposed her beliefs. In November 1637, she was ordered to appear before the General Court.

Winthrop served as the colony's main lawyer for the hearing. He questioned Hutchinson about her actions and beliefs. He said she had "troubled the peace of the commonwealth and the churches here." Hutchinson chose not to have a lawyer. She would defend herself. In her articulate style, she proclaimed to the court that she was merely following her conscience and not trying to break the law. She also shocked the court by declaring that she had heard a voice from God that told her what to do. The Puritans

Anne Hutchinson preached to her followers at meetings she held in her home.

believed that God no longer spoke directly to humans, as they believed God did in the days of the Bible.

At the end of the trial, the General Court found Hutchinson guilty. She was banished from Massachusetts with her family and 60 of her followers. Several others who stayed lost their right to vote. Fearing future trouble, leaders took away the guns of any resident who had supported Hutchinson or Wheelwright.

The community and its leaders soon received what they thought was a sign from God—confirmation that they had made the right decision to expel Hutchinson and her followers. A story was spreading that Hutchinson, a midwife, had once delivered a dead baby that was a monster. People were saying that the baby had no head, its ears and eyes were on its body, and above its eyes were four hard horns. Hutchinson and one other woman were the only ones who saw the baby before it was buried, the story went. The Puritans believed that God had punished the Antinomians by creating this horrible creature.

The Antinomian problem was probably the worst crisis Winthrop faced as governor. The disputes in and around Boston threatened to split apart both the church and the colony. Some people, especially Shepard and Dudley, wanted more people punished. In particular, they disliked the part John Cotton had played in the crisis. Once a defender of Hutchinson, Cotton later turned strongly against her as the trial went on. As he had always done, Winthrop tried to take a forgiving path and still deal justly with the worst offenders, such as Hutchinson.

The Hutchinson trial led Winthrop to do

Puritans in Massachusetts Bay Colony were sometimes punished by being placed in stocks.

something he had not done in years—he wrote in his journal about his own religious experience. The crisis, he wrote, led him "to examine my own [state]. ... My heart opened up to let [Jesus Christ] in. Oh, how I was ravished with his love!" Winthrop then wrote a complete history of his religious life. He called it his "Christian Experience." Winthrop's faith had helped him survive many things. Other challenges still awaited him and his colony. ✑

8 TROUBLE IN ENGLAND

❦

At the end of the Hutchinson trial, winter arrived with a fury. A thick blanket of snow covered the ground and stayed there through March 1638. Snow fell again in late April. In May, Winthrop came down with a high fever that brought him near death. It took a month for him to recover and get back to serving as governor.

New settlers arrived that year. Others moved on to Rhode Island or other nearby settlements. Winthrop kept busy with a variety of duties. As part of the General Court, he gave land to colonists, granted permission for new towns to form, made treaties with Indians, collected taxes, and handled legal affairs.

Although the Puritans tried to lead good lives, some residents still broke the law. The crimes ranged

A Puritan governor interrupts the colonists for unlawfully taking part in sports activities on Christmas Day.

from swearing to being drunk in public to murder. Winthrop noted in his journal that one woman was executed for killing her young daughter. He wrote that she was "so possessed with Satan that he persuaded her ... to break the neck of her own child." The colonists saw either God's or the devil's influence in most of their activities. "[T]he devil would never cease to disturb our peace," Winthrop once wrote.

Winthrop spent a great deal of time handling the affairs of the colony. But he also had to deal with personal problems, most of them financial. It had been five years since he had hired a man named James Luxford to run his farm. Over the years, Luxford cheated Winthrop, got him deeply in debt, and participated in illegal business deals.

Although Luxford was brought to court and banished from the colony, his punishment didn't end Winthrop's financial problems. In 1640, members of several churches helped Winthrop by giving him money. But the demands of paying his debts convinced him that he should give up some of his government duties. When some Puritan leaders suggested it was time for a new governor, Winthrop agreed not to run again and to serve as an assistant.

To help pay off his debts, Winthrop sold his large Boston mansion and moved into a smaller house. He also sold some of his land. Some Massachusetts residents disliked Winthrop for the power he had

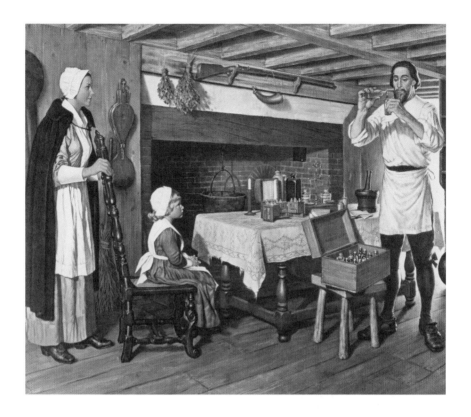

gained over the years. They used this opportunity to suggest that Winthrop's money problems were a punishment from God. Yet he still had the support of most of the colonists, because in 1642, voters once again elected him as their governor.

By this time, Massachusetts Bay settlers were paying close attention to what had been brewing in England over the past four years. Religion was at the heart of an intensifying conflict between England and Scotland. King Charles I wanted the Scots to follow the rules of the Church of England. But most Scots

In addition to farming and govern- ing, Winthrop performed pharmaceutical services in his home.

were Calvinists—opposed to the Church of England and its policies.

Scottish forces invaded England in 1639, and Parliament took control of the English government away from the king. Many of the king's aides were arrested, including William Laud, who had actively persecuted English Puritans for many years. By 1642, the British were fighting against each other. On one side of the civil war were Calvinists and those who supported the power of Parliament. On the other side were people who were loyal to the king and the Church of England.

Supporters of Parliament destroyed royal property in protest against the king of England.

Although the clash was an ocean away, it affected Massachusetts Bay. Puritans stopped coming to New England since the war made travel difficult. Some colonists returned to their homeland, believing that Calvinists would win the battle and the Church of England would be based on Calvinist beliefs.

Massachusetts Bay residents were also hearing about problems in other colonies. Winthrop reported that "Indians all over the country had combined themselves" and planned to "kill them [colonial leaders] in the houses and seize their weapons." Winthrop and the General Court sent men to take weapons away from local Indians before they could attack. Winthrop and leaders of three other Puritan colonies then decided to join together to defend themselves. In 1643, they formed the United Colonies of New England. The colonists, however, were never attacked. They continued to have mostly peaceful relations with the Indians.

As the threat of an Indian war passed, trouble arrived in Boston. In June 1643, a French ship entered

> The United Colonies of New England included Massachusetts Bay, Plymouth, Connecticut, and New Haven, which later became part of Connecticut. It was created to preserve and spread the gospel found in the Bible and for the mutual safety and welfare of the colonies. Massachusetts, the largest of the four, was required to provide the most soldiers. Each colony sent two representatives to a governing body. The United Colonies became an example and model for the government of the United States.

Charles la Tour and his father Claude played important roles in settling Nova Scotia, Canada.

Boston Harbor and asked to land. In charge of the ship was Charles La Tour and another Frenchman who were struggling for control of French Acadia—now Nova Scotia, Canada. La Tour asked for Winthrop's

help. The governor called a meeting of some of the leaders, who said La Tour could come on shore and recruit men and ships.

Soon Winthrop's critics were at work. They did not like the idea of helping France, a longtime enemy of England. Most French were Roman Catholics, the religious enemies of the Puritans. Winthrop told his foes he was following the Bible's command to love your neighbor as you love yourself. Later, Winthrop admitted he had made a mistake. He said he should have talked to all the leaders and then called upon God, as they usually did before they discussed any issue.

A letter from John Endecott showed how the La Tour affair hurt Winthrop: "[Y]our troubles are many, and especially about this French business." Winthrop's troubles as governor were far from over. ॐ

John Endecott was governor of Salem when John Winthrop arrived in the New World.

JOHN WINTHROP

9 BATTLING FOES IN HIS FINAL DAYS

Chapter

❦

Despite the criticisms, voters continued to trust John Winthrop. In 1644, he was elected deputy governor, and John Endecott became governor. On the other hand, some people in Massachusetts still felt the governor and his assistants had too much power. These critics thought their local representatives in the General Court, called deputies, should have much more influence.

Many leaders and colonists didn't like how people were complaining. They called them the "negative voice." Winthrop, however, defended them. The foundations of government would be overthrown "if this negative voice be layed down," he wrote. Some people also accused magistrates, or judges, of the General Court of having arbitrary power—acting

A marble statue of John Winthrop stands in Statuary Hall in the U.S. Capitol.

as they chose without listening to the voters. Now Winthrop stated:

> [W]here the people have the liberty to admit or reject their governors, and to require the rule by which they should be governed and judged, this is not arbitrary government.

The arguments over government were still going on in 1645. In the town of Hingham, Anthony Eames and Bozoan Allen wanted the leaders of the colony to choose which one would be the main leader of the local militia. The magistrates said Eames should be captain. The deputies and most townspeople, however, favored Allen. Eventually, some of Allen's supporters were arrested, and they blamed Winthrop for it.

The charge of arbitrary power was once again on the lips of many Massachusetts Bay residents. Allen's supporters brought Winthrop to court, accusing him of illegally putting citizens in jail. They hoped to force Winthrop out of office.

The colony was facing its toughest political struggle since the Anne Hutchinson case of 1637. Winthrop's foes in Hingham were trying to weaken the rule of the Massachusetts Bay Company and give local towns more power. The trial became a direct assault on Winthrop. To his critics, Winthrop was the symbol of arbitrary power.

For days, the courtroom was filled with angry voices. Many deputies agreed that Winthrop had too much power, but most magistrates supported Winthrop. In the end, he was found innocent. Before the trial ended, Winthrop asked to speak. He gave what he called "a little speech." It became one of his most famous public speeches.

Members of the General Court heard testimony against citizens as well as government officials like John Winthrop.

In it, Winthrop clearly stated his beliefs about government. He said voters chose the magistrates, who have their authority from God. The magistrates agree to govern the people and judge their causes by the rules of God's law and their own. They judge to the best of their ability, he said, but they are human— they make mistakes and have the same flaws as any other person.

Winthrop went on to talk about two kinds of liberty: natural and civil. In nature, he said, man has

John Winthrop believed people had the right to choose their own leaders but then had the responsibility to obey them.

the freedom to do whatever he wants, both good and evil. But in a society, "[i]t is a liberty to that only which is good, just, and honest." Civil liberty requires obeying elected officials, he proclaimed. People have the freedom to be a part of a community and elect magistrates. But that liberty also requires them to follow the magistrates' orders.

When General Court ended in May, Winthrop noted that the magistrates and deputies "departed in much love." Winthrop's words must have had some impact, because the following year, voters once again elected him governor. He would hold that position for the rest of his life.

Some residents continued to insist on changes in the colony. They claimed that a recent outbreak of disease and financial problems were punishments from God. The Lord, they declared, opposed the negative voice and arbitrary power of the magistrates. The petition asked that all citizens be made members of local churches. That way, everyone would meet the requirements to be a freeman and would have the right to vote.

In November, Winthrop and the General Court decided to ignore the petition. The men who wrote it said they would take their concerns to the English Parliament. But as one of the petitioners prepared to set sail for London, he was arrested. The magistrates seized his papers that related to the petition.

About the same time, the General Court selected Edward Winslow to go to England to make sure Massachusetts could keep its charter. The next year, in 1647, the colony was given the go-ahead from England to continue governing itself as it always had. This good news was just what Winthrop wanted. But there was also bad news that year.

In the spring, an epidemic went through the colony, and in June, it killed Margaret. The governor

Edward Winslow (1595–1655) represented Massachusetts Bay in England when the colony's charter came up for renewal.

wrote in his journal that his wife was "specially beloved and honored of all the country." Winthrop's children were not in Massachusetts at the time, so he dealt with his wife's sickness and death without the support of his family.

Winthrop's love for Margaret had always been strong. Still, he did not want to spend his last years alone. A few months later, in December, he married Martha Coytmore. Winthrop would have only a brief time to enjoy his fourth marriage, however. He was sick with a fever for six weeks in 1648. In spite of being ill, he kept up with the affairs of the colony. But in February 1649, Winthrop again became ill. This time he was too weak to get out of bed.

On March 14, Adam Winthrop wrote to his brother John that their father was "brought very low, weaker than I ever knew him." Thomas Dudley visited Winthrop often. They were friends now, having settled their differences when Winthrop's daughter Mary and Dudley's son Samuel had married.

Dudley was still tending to the affairs of the colony and trying to enforce strict punishments. Even as Winthrop lay ill, Dudley asked him to sign an order banishing someone who rejected Puritan beliefs. Winthrop, in his typical compassionate style, refused to sign it. He told Dudley that "he had done too much of that work already."

On March 26, 1649, Governor John Winthrop died

in his Boston home at the age of 61. He was buried next to Margaret. The firing of guns saluted him in his death.

The person who led the largest migration of colonists to North America was now gone. Over time, Winthrop's idea of a city upon a hill influenced many Americans. They applied the image to the United States of America. Some believed God had chosen Americans for a special mission—to spread freedom and democracy and set an example for the rest of the world. President Ronald Reagan (1911–2004) was one of many leaders who referred to Winthrop's city upon a hill as the ideal for the United States. The words showed how important Winthrop and the Puritans were in shaping America.

During his life, John Winthrop made some enemies and sometimes denied citizens the freedom they craved. Yet he always believed he was acting as God wanted and in the best interests of the colony. He tried to balance the needs of various people and groups and still rule the colony with fairness and mercy. Under Winthrop's leadership, no English residents had greater

England's civil war ended in 1649, the year John Winthrop died. But Winthrop had already died when news reached Massachusetts Bay Colony that Parliament had executed King Charles I. A Puritan named Oliver Cromwell had led the efforts to get rid of the king. Cromwell then ruled England until 1658 under the title Lord Protector.

John Winthrop is buried next to his third wife, Margaret, in Boston, Massachusetts.

democracy than the settlers of Massachusetts.

Today, more people know about the city upon the hill than the wise and caring man who spoke those words. As one modern historian said, John Winthrop was America's first great man.

WINTHROP'S LIFE

1588

Born on January 12 in Edwardston, Suffolk, England

1602

Attends school at Cambridge University

1600

1588

The English navy and merchant ships defeat the Spanish armada off the coast of France

1603

James I becomes king of England and Ireland

WORLD EVENTS

1605

Marries Mary Forth; leaves Cambridge University without graduating

1611

Attends Gray's Inn to study law

1615

Appointed justice of the peace; wife Mary dies

1610

1607

Jamestown, Virginia, the first English settlement on the North American mainland, is founded

1611

The King James Bible, commissioned by the British king, is published

1614

Pocahontas marries John Rolfe

Life and Times

WINTHROP'S LIFE

1627

Appointed by English
government to serve
on royal court

1618

Marries Margaret
Tyndal

1625

1620

The *Mayflower* with
its Pilgrim passengers
sails from England to
North America

1624

England declares
war on Spain

1628

John Bunyan,
popular English
religious author,
is born

WORLD EVENTS

1629

Elected governor
of the colony in
Massachusetts

1630

Sets sail for
Massachusetts;
delivers sermon "A
Model of Christian
Charity"

1636

Banishes Roger
Williams from
Massachusetts Bay
Colony

1630

1632

King Charles I
issues a charter
for the colony
of Maryland

1635

English High
and Latin
School, Boston,
Massachusetts,
oldest second-
ary school in
North America,
is founded

1629

Empress Meisho
ascends to the
throne of Japan

WINTHROP'S LIFE

1643

Helps create the United Colonies of New England

1637

Confronts Anne Hutchinson in court

1639

Sells land to pay for huge debt caused by his farm manager

1640

1638

Louis XIV, future king of France, is born

1642

Isaac Newton, English mathematician and philosopher, is born

WORLD EVENTS

1645
Defends himself and the Massachusetts Bay Colony's government during his trial

1647
Wife Margaret dies; marries Martha Coytmore

1649
Dies on March 26; buried in Boston, Massachusetts

1645
Jeanne Mance founds a hospital in Montreal, the first in North America

1646
English occupy the Bahamas

1649
Puritan exiles from Virginia settle in Providence, Maryland, near present-day Annapolis

DATE OF BIRTH: January 12, 1588

BIRTHPLACE: Edwardston, England

FATHER: Adam Winthrop
(1548–1623)

MOTHER: Anne Browne Winthrop
(1558–1629)

EDUCATION: Cambridge University

FIRST SPOUSE: Mary Forth (1583–1615)

CHILDREN: John Jr. (1606–1676)
Henry (1608–1630)
Forth (1609–1630)
Mary (1612–1643)
Anne (1614)
Anne (1615)

SECOND SPOUSE: Thomasine Clopton
(1583–1616)

THIRD SPOUSE: Margaret Tyndal
(1591–1647)

CHILDREN: Stephen (1619–1658)
Adam (1620–1652)
Deane (1623–1704)
Samuel (1627–1674)
Anne (1630-1631)

FOURTH SPOUSE: Martha Coytmore
(?–1660)

DATE OF DEATH: March 26, 1649

PLACE OF BURIAL: Boston, Massachusetts

FURTHER READING

Aronson, Marc. *John Winthrop, Oliver Cromwell, and the Land of Promise.* New York: Clarion Books, 2004.

Connelly, Elizabeth Russell. *John Winthrop: Politician and Statesman.* Philadelphia: Chelsea House Publishers, 2001.

Gaustad, Edwin S. *Roger Williams: Prophet of Liberty.* New York: Oxford University Press, 2001.

Kent, Deborah. *In Colonial New England.* New York: Benchmark Books, 1999.

Newman, Shirlee Petkin. *The Pequots.* New York: Franklin Watts, 2000.

Slavicek, Louise Chipley. *Life Among the Puritans.* San Diego: Lucent Books, 2001.

Wiener, Roberta, and James R. Arnold. *Massachusetts: The History of Massachusetts Colony, 1620–1776.* Chicago: Raintree, 2005.

LOOK FOR MORE SIGNATURE LIVES BOOKS ABOUT THIS ERA:

Lord Baltimore: *Founder of Maryland*
ISBN 0-7565-1592-0

Anne Hutchinson: *Puritan Protester*
ISBN 0-7565-1577-7

William Penn: *Founder of Pennsylvania*
ISBN 0-7565-1598-X

Roger Williams: *Founder of Rhode Island*
ISBN 0-7565-1596-3

ON THE WEB

For more information on *John Winthrop*, use FactHound.

1. Go to *www.facthound.com*
2. Type in a search word related to this book or this book ID: 0756515912
3. Click on the *Fetch It* button.

FactHound will fetch the best Web sites for you.

HISTORIC SITES

City Square Park
Charlestown, Massachusetts
Site of an archaeological dig that unearthed the postholes and outline of John Winthrop's house

Boston National Historical Park
Charlestown Navy Yard
Boston, MA 02129
617/242-5642
A walking tour of the historical sites in the city of Boston

arbitrary
based on an individual's decision rather than
according to law

banished
forced to leave a community

bishops
religious leaders in charge of churches in a region

charter
an official document granting permission to set up
a new organization or colony

gentry
landowners in England who made up the upper
social classes

impeachment
a process for charging a government official with
misconduct while in office

magistrates
government officials who make and enforce laws

migration
movement of people from one area to another

militia
an army made up of private citizens who serve
during military emergencies

persecution
cruel or unfair treatment of a group of people, for
example, because of their religious beliefs

sedition
actions or words meant to stir up rebellion against
a government

Chapter 1

Page 9, line 3: "Shipboard Journal of John Winthrop." The Winthrop Society. 13 October 2005. www.winthropsociety.org/journal.php.

Page 9, line 11: Ibid.

Page 12, line 4: John Winthrop, Richard S. Dunn, and Laetitia Yeandle. *The Journal of John Winthrop 1630-1649*. Abridged ed. Cambridge, Mass.: Belknap Press of Harvard University, 1996, p. 10.

Page 12, line 9: "A Modell of Christian Charity." Wikisource. 13 October 2005. http://en.wikisource.org/wiki/City_upon_a_Hill.

Page 13, line 5: "Shipboard Journal of John Winthrop," p. 6.

Chapter 2

Page 21, line 10: Francis J. Bremer. *John Winthrop: America's Forgotten Founding Father*. New York: Oxford University Press, 2003, p. 70.

Page 21, line 21: Robert C. Winthrop. *Life and Letters of John Winthrop, Governor of the Massachusetts-Bay Company at Their Emigration to New England*, Vol. 1. Boston: Ticknor and Fields, 1864-1867, pp. 56-57.

Page 22, line 17: Ibid.

Chapter 3

Page 25, line 10: Ibid., p. 66.

Page 27, line 3: Ibid., p. 73.

Page 27, line 9: Ibid., p. 105.

Page 27, line 13: *John Winthrop: America's Forgotten Founding Father*, p. 103.

Page 29, line 3: Ibid., p. 115.

Page 30, line 23: Ibid., p. 140.

Page 32, line 4: Darrett Bruce Rutman. *John Winthrop's Decision for America: 1629*. Philadelphia: Lippincott, 1975, p. 65.

Page 34, line 14: *Life and Letters of John Winthrop, Governor of the Massachusetts-Bay Company at Their Emigration to New England*, Vol. 1, p. 228.

Page 35, line 24: Ibid., p. 283.

Page 36, line 3: *John Winthrop's Decision for America: 1629*, p. 80.

Page 38, line 14: *John Winthrop: America's Forgotten Founding Father*, p. 155.

Page 40, line 5: *John Winthrop's Decision for America: 1629*, p. 87.

Page 41, line 16: *John Winthrop: America's Forgotten Founding Father*, p. 160.

Page 41, line 21: *Life and Letters of John Winthrop, Governor of the Massachusetts-Bay Company at Their Emigration to New England*, Vol. 1, p. 340.

Chapter 4

Page 45, line 4: Ibid., p. 356.

Page 45, line 12: Ibid., p. 379.

Page 46, line 19: *The Journal of John Winthrop 1630-1649*, p. 16.

Page 49, line 19: *Life and Letters of John Winthrop, Governor of the Massachusetts-Bay Company at Their Emigration to New England*, Vol. 2, p. 30.

Chapter 5

Page 60, line 5: *The Journal of John Winthrop 1630-1649*, p. 50.

Page 61, line 13: Ibid., p. 89.

Chapter 6

Page 66, line 1: Ibid., p. 28.

Page 67, line 8: Ibid., pp. 74-75.

Chapter 7

Page 73, line 6: Ibid., p. 105.

Page 73, line 22: Ibid., p. 115.

Page 74, line 21: "Trial at the Court at Newton." Annehutchinson.com. 14 October 2005. http://www.annehutchinson.com/anne_hutchinson_trial_001.html.

Page 77, line 3: *Life and Letters of John Winthrop, Governor of the Massachusetts-Bay Company at Their Emigration to New England*, Vol. 2, p. 161.

Chapter 8

Page 80, line 4: *The Journal of John Winthrop 1630-1649*, p. 148.

Page 80, line 7: Ibid., p. 149.

Page 83, line 9: Ibid., p. 211.

Page 85, line 21: *John Winthrop: America's Forgotten Founding Father*, p. 346.

Chapter 9

Page 87, line 12: *Life and Letters of John Winthrop, Governor of the Massachusetts-Bay Company at Their Emigration to New England*, Vol. 2, p. 438.

Page 88, line 3: *John Winthrop: America's Forgotten Founding Father*, p. 359.

Page 91, line 2: *The Journal of John Winthrop 1630-1649*, pp. 282-283.

Page 91, line 9: Ibid., p. 296.

Page 93, line 1: Ibid., p. 328.

Page 93, line 16: *Life and Letters of John Winthrop, Governor of the Massachusetts-Bay Company at Their Emigration to New England*, Vol. 2, p. 391.

Page 93, line 26: Ibid., p. 393.

Ashley, Maurice. *England in the Seventeenth Century*. London: Penguin, 1975.

Bremer, Francis J. *John Winthrop: America's Forgotten Founding Father*. New York: Oxford University Press, 2003.

Faragher, John Mack, ed. *The Encyclopedia of Colonial and Revolutionary America*. New York: Da Capo Press, 1996.

Gaustad, Edwin S. *Liberty of Conscience: Roger Williams in America*. Valley Forge, Pa.: Judson Press, 1999.

Labaree, Benjamin Woods *Colonial Massachusetts: A History*. Millwood, N.Y.: KTO Press, 1979.

Morgan, Edmund Sears. *The Genuine Article: A Historian Looks at Early America*. New York: W.W. Norton & Co., 2004.

Morgan, Edmund Sears. *The Puritan Dilemma: The Story of John Winthrop*. Boston: Little, Brown, 1958.

Moseley, James G. *John Winthrop's World: History as a Story; The Story as History*. Madison: University of Wisconsin Press, 1992.

Rutman, Darrett Bruce. *John Winthrop's Decision for America: 1629*. Philadelphia: Lippincott, 1975.

Waldman, Carl, ed. *Atlas of the North American Indian*. New York: Checkmark Books, 2000.

Winslow, Ola Elizabeth. *Master Roger Williams: A Biography*. New York: MacMillan, 1957.

Winthrop, John, Richard S. Dunn, and Laetitia Yeandle. *The Journal of John Winthrop, 1630–1649*. Abridged ed. Cambridge, Mass.: Belknap Press of Harvard University, 1996.

Winthrop, Robert C. *Life and Letters of John Winthrop, Governor of the Massachusetts-Bay Company at Their Emigration to New England*. 2 vols. Boston: Ticknor and Fields, 1864–1867.

Michael Burgan is a freelance writer of books for children and adults. A history graduate of the University of Connecticut, he has written more than 90 fiction and nonfiction children's books. For adult audiences, he has written news articles, essays, and plays. Michael Burgan is a recipient of an Educational Press Association of America award.

Image Credits

North Wind Picture Archives, cover (top), 4–5, 8, 19, 47, 51, 60, 63, 64, 69, 72, 85, 99 (top right); The Granger Collection, New York, cover (bottom), 2, 23, 24, 27, 29, 31, 54, 66, 77, 78, 89, 92, 99 (top left); Stapleton Collection/Corbis, 11; Lombard Antiquarian Maps & Prints, 12, 96 (top); From *The Founding of New England* by James Truslow Adams, 14; Mary Evans Picture Library, 16, 20, 58, 82, 84; Rischgitz/Getty Images, 32; Fitzwilliam Museum, University of Cambridge, UK/The Bridgeman Art Library, 33; Massachusetts Historical Society, Boston, Massachusetts/The Bridgeman Art Library, 35; Time & Life Pictures/Getty Images, 37; Hulton Archive/Getty Images, 39, 96 (bottom left); Bettmann/Corbis, 42, 48, 57, 70, 75, 100 (top left); Winchester Public Library/Photo by Norton Photography, 52–53; MPI/Getty Images, 59, 100 (top right); Private Collection/The Bridgeman Art Library, 73, 81; Architect of the Capitol, 86, 101 (top); Stock Montage/Getty Images, 90; Robert Holmes/Corbis, 95; Library of Congress, 96 (bottom right), 98 (all), 99 (bottom), 100 (bottom, all); National Parks Service/Colonial National Historical Park, 97 (left); Kean Collection/Getty Images, 97 (right); Canadian Heritage Gallery #10126/Sophia Louisa Elliott/National Archives of Canada C-3202, 101 (bottom).